Developing Literacy
POETRY

READING AND WRITING
ACTIVITIES FOR THE LITERACY HOUR

year

Christine Moorcroft

Series consultant Ray Barker

A & C BLACK

Contents

Humorous verse

Theme and meaning

Acknowledgements

The author and publishers are grateful for permission to reproduce the following:

p. 9 'The Horseman' by Walter de la Mare, reproduced with permission of the Literary Trustees of Walter de la Mare, and the Society of Authors as their representative; p. 18 'Green Lettuce, Green Peas' from *Colours* © 1986 Shirley Hughes. Reproduced by permission of the publisher Walker Books Ltd., London; p. 25 'De Beat' by Grace Nichols, reproduced with permission of Curtis Brown Ltd, London, on behalf of Grace Nichols. Copyright Grace Nichols 1998; p. 28 'Jump or Jiggle' by Evelyn Beyer, from *Another Here and Now Story Book* by Lucy Sprague Mitchell, copyright 1937 by E.P. Dutton, renewed © 1965 by Lucy Sprague Mitchell. Used by permission of Dutton Children's Books, an imprint of Penguin Putnam Books for Young Readers, a division of Penguin Putnam Inc; p. 44 'Ducks' Ditty' from *The Wind in the Willows* by Kenneth Grahame. Copyright The University Chest, Oxford, reproduced by permission of Curtis Brown Ltd., London.

Published 2001 by
A & C Black (Publishers) Limited
37 Soho Square, London W1D 3QZ

ISBN 0-7136-5868-1

The author and publishers would like to thank Ray Barker, Madeleine Madden, Kim Pérez and Julia Tappin for their advice in producing this series of books.

A CIP catalogue record for this book is available from the British Library.

Printed in Great Britain by Caligraving Ltd, Thetford, Norfolk.

Introduction

Developing Literacy: Poetry is a series of seven photocopiable activity books for the Literacy Hour. Each book provides a range of poetry activities for the Literacy Hour, and supports the teaching of reading and writing skills at text, sentence and word levels. The books contain more than enough ideas for the year for which they are intended, and provide teachers with a range of activities to select from.

The activities are designed to be carried out in the time allocated to independent work and incorporate strategies that encourage independent learning – for example, ways in which children can evaluate their own work or that of a partner.

The activities in **Year 2** encourage children to:

- develop their enjoyment of poems with familiar settings, poems by significant children's poets, poems from different cultures, poems with predictable and patterned language and poems with language play and other humorous devices;

- recite poems;

- experiment with words, sounds, rhymes and rhythms;

- compose their own poems and rhymes, based on the structures of, and using some of the devices in, those that they read, with the aid of the frameworks provided.

The National Literacy Strategy and poetry

The National Literacy Strategy *Framework for Teaching* encourages teachers to read all kinds of poetry and verse with children, including playground chants, nursery rhymes, action rhymes, advertisements and jingles as well as more formal poetry. The text-level objectives include teaching *about* poetry – different types of poetry, the devices used by poets, the 'messages' of poems and even the shapes of poems, plus many of the technical terms associated with poetry. Research also indicates that the ability to appreciate rhyme and rhythm has a positive effect on children's learning to read and spell, and that several

word-level objectives can be successfully taught *through* poetry: the use of rhyme to teach about phonics and onset and rime, and of rhythm to teach about syllables.

However, teachers should not lose sight of the fun of poetry – the 'playing with words' of poets like Roger McGough and the clever use of humour by poets like Charles Causley and E V Rieu. In poetry, children can ignore the rules of grammar and put words together in new ways. And, as with other kinds of writing, the children can learn from experts. The teacher's role is to help the children recognise a particular form of poetry, to provide a structure to help them write it, and to help them identify and practise the devices used by poets so that they can use them in their own poems.

Using poetry in the Literacy Hour

This book focuses on the independent part of the Literacy Hour but the notes on pages 6–8 and at the foot of each activity page suggest a variety of ways in which to introduce poetry lessons, present whole-class activities and use plenary sessions to conclude the lessons. Teachers will find it useful to vary their approaches, and could also try some of the following, as appropriate for their year group:

- playing professional tape-recordings of poems;

- choral speaking by individuals, small or large groups, and the whole class;

- learning poems a line or two at a time (varying the tone and expression as appropriate);

- reciting poems which have been learned;

- enacting, miming or singing poems;

- listing rhymes, alliterative or onomatopoeic words;

- clapping, tapping or stamping rhythms;

- making lists of words on a topic;

- composing poems as a group or class;

- holding small-group discussions and open forums during which the children discuss poems they have read or written.

Listening to poems

This book includes poems which need to be read to, and with, the children. Children in Year 2 can understand poems which they cannot read without help, for example, extracts from works by Shakespeare. By listening to poems that they would be unable to read for themselves, the children can learn to enjoy the ideas, stories and feelings expressed in such poems, as well as the sounds, rhymes and rhythms. This lays the foundations on which they can model their own poems. Listening to the poets themselves or actors reading aloud can be of special value in helping the children to enjoy a poem. At the same time, the children learn how to read poetry aloud themselves. School television programmes on poetry could be used, as could commercially available tapes: for example, *Poetry Please* and *The Nation's Favourite Poems* (BBC) and *The Penguin Book of English Verse* (Penguin Classics).

Giving the children the printed work to follow enables them to memorise some of the words, even if they cannot read them, and to recognise them when they come across them again.

Reading poems aloud

Several activities in this book ask the children to read poems aloud (both their own and those of other poets). This helps them to appreciate the poem's meaning, atmosphere and rhythm; and in the case of their own poems, to think of changes which might improve them. Sometimes, the notes that accompany an activity suggest ways in which the poems can be read aloud (for example, individuals, pairs, or small or large groups can read the parts of different characters or individual lines, groups of lines, verses and choruses). The way in which a poem is spoken can make a valuable contribution to the children's understanding, appreciation and enjoyment of it, so you might experiment with different methods, depending on the poem: for example, a poem with a quiet atmosphere might be spoken using a combination of solo voices and hushed combined voices; the rhythm of a train might be created by having one group beginning to read a line while another group is finishing the previous line.

Memorising poems

Many of the activities in this book suggest that the children memorise a poem, rhyme or verse. When they memorise poetry, the children increase their vocabulary and develop the skill of using it expressively; they build up a rich store of creative ways in which words can be used, and they begin to use them themselves.

To help the children memorise a poem, read it aloud to them, then repeat it, encouraging them to join in. Either display an enlarged copy of the poem, or work with a small group of children who each have their own copy to follow. Read a line, then cover it and ask the children to repeat it, gradually building up the number of lines covered until the children can recite the entire poem.

The following mnemonic reminds the children how they can learn a poem:

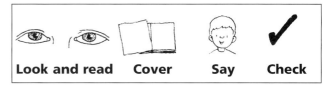

Organisation

The activities require very few resources besides scissors, glue, word-banks and simple dictionaries. Other materials are specified in the teachers' notes on the pages.

Extension activities

Most of the activity sheets end with a challenge (**Now try this!**) which reinforces and extends the children's learning and provides the teacher with an opportunity for assessment. These more challenging activities might be appropriate for only a few children; it is not expected that the whole class should complete all of them. On some pages there is space for the children to complete the extension activities, but others will require a notebook or separate sheet of paper.

Notes on the activities

The notes below expand upon those that are provided at the foot of each activity page. They give ideas and suggestions for making the most of the activity sheet, including suggestions for the whole-class introduction, the plenary session or for follow-up work using an adapted version of the activity sheet. To help teachers select appropriate learning experiences for their pupils, the activities are grouped into sections within each book, but the pages need not be presented in the order in which they appear, unless otherwise stated.

Poems for reading aloud, learning, enjoying and repeating

The poems in this section should be read aloud by the children, either taking turns during the introductory session or in groups. Give them opportunities to experiment with different ways of reading the poems aloud (including different numbers of voices for different parts of the poem), and encourage them to look out for repeated parts, such as choruses, which could be read by the whole group.

The horseman (page 9). This is a poem for the children to read aloud and to memorise. They should notice the rhyming words. In the first two lines, point out the words which begin with the same sound: 'heard', 'horseman' and 'hill'. Talk about the atmosphere of the poem and ask the children what kind of picture it makes them imagine.

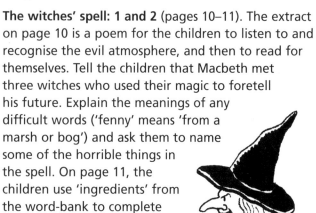

The witches' spell: 1 and 2 (pages 10–11). The extract on page 10 is a poem for the children to listen to and recognise the evil atmosphere, and then to read for themselves. Tell the children that Macbeth met three witches who used their magic to foretell his future. Explain the meanings of any difficult words ('fenny' means 'from a marsh or bog') and ask them to name some of the horrible things in the spell. On page 11, the children use 'ingredients' from the word-bank to complete the First Witch's spell.

The effects of words

The activities in this section develop the children's appreciation of the ways in which poets use words to create effects.

Word-pictures: 1 and 2 (pages 12–13). To introduce the activity, display poems and draw attention to evocative lines or groups of words. The words could be copied and displayed in enlarged form. Discuss the images that the words conjure up and encourage the children to describe and draw these images. The extracts on page 12 are from *The Listeners* (Walter de la Mare), *Shining Things* (Elizabeth Gould), *I Saw* (Anon) and *My Sari* (Debjanee Chatterjee). Page 13 helps the children to create their own 'word-pictures', by providing a structure on which they can make notes about their observations, write a description based on their notes, highlight the most important words and then write a short 'word-picture'.

Sad sounds, happy sounds (page 14) develops the children's appreciation of the ways in which poets create effects to convey feelings. The extracts are from: *Ode to a Nightingale* (John Keats), *Everyone Sang* (Siegfried Sassoon), *Come on into my Tropical Garden* (Grace Nichols), *Farewell Address* (Chief Plenty Coups, leader of the Crow people) and *Daffodils* (William Wordsworth).

Sad words, happy words (page 15) develops the children's skills in making and organising notes and jottings to use in their own poems. Encourage them to look for sad and happy words in other poems.

Poets' words (page 16) could be introduced through the poems of Lewis Carroll (who invented 'slithy') or Edward Lear (who invented 'runcible spoon'), as well as those of modern poets like Colin West (who invented the phrase 'at a total lossage' to describe his feelings when trying to find a rhyme for 'sausage'!).

Your own words (page 17) helps the children to invent their own words. Before this activity is presented, a 'word-factory' could be set up in the classroom – a table and display area containing materials to stimulate the creation of new words: for example, illustrated examples of made-up words (like those on the activity sheet) and words invented by writers of stories and poems, along with old words which are no longer used (such as ones coined by Shakespeare).

Green poem and **Red poem** (pages 18–19). Before the lessons, the children could keep notebooks in which to make jottings about anything they see that is green (or red). They could take turns to name green things: 'Green leaves, green string, green buds,' and so on (or red things: 'Red car, red ball, red shoes,' and so on).

Rhythm

The activities in this section help the children to recognise different types of rhythms and to develop their appreciation of the effects of these rhythms. The children are also encouraged to explore the rhythms they hear in everyday life.

Pattern poem (page 20). During the plenary session, the children could take turns around the class to read a line from their poems. They could decide which lines could be combined to make a class poem.

Chat poem (page 21). Read (or sing) the lines of the following traditional rhyme, stopping at the asterisks for the children to try to supply the missing words:

See you later, *alligator. / In a while *crocodile. / See you later, hot *potato. / If you wish, *jellyfish.

This can be linked with work on rhyme and with word-level work on the different spellings of similar sounds.

The way you say it: 1 and 2 (pages 22–23). The counting poem on page 22 should be read aloud with a 'counting' rhythm. Ask the children to notice where the pauses are. How do the pauses help them to count? Can they work out how the numbers between 11 and 19 are formed? Some children might also be able to work out the names for 21 to 29 and invent a word for 30. On page 23, the children make up their own words for numbers. During the plenary session, ask them to explain how they chose the words.

Aliens' alphabet (page 24). The children should first write out and recite the normal English alphabet, noticing which letters rhyme (a, j, k and b, c, d, e, g, p, t, v). Encourage the children to try to make the corresponding letters in the aliens' alphabet rhyme; they could also make the names for them begin with the same sounds as their corresponding letters in the English alphabet (for example, ag, bag, cag, dag, eag). Ask them to recite their alphabets.

The drum (page 25). This poem has the rhythm of drumbeats, making the drum seem to be a living thing. The children could identify the words and phrases which contribute to this effect ('skin', 'belly', 'a living heart', 'a living goat', 'a living tree').

Rhyme

These activities encourage the children to explore rhyme for its own sake and to enjoy the sounds of words. They also develop the children's appreciation of different rhyme patterns.

Rhyme match: 1 and 2 (pages 26–27) are based on the traditional skipping rhyme:

> Up and down, up and down,
> All the way to London Town.
> Heel and toe, heel and toe,
> All the way to Jericho.
> Swish swash, swish swash,
> All the way to Charing Cross.

The last two lines have been changed to avoid half-rhymes, but these could be introduced to children who are ready for them. Some children might be able to make up their own verses.

Hump, jump, wiggle, jiggle and **Crash, dash, rumble, tumble** (pages 28–29) encourage the children to look for rhymes that make sense: they consider the ways in which the animals move, find the right words for these movements and then arrange them in rhyming pairs. This can be linked with word-level work on vocabulary extension (interesting words for movement to replace 'go'/'goes' and 'went') and with phonological awareness (onset and rime, phonemes and word endings).

Alliterative patterns

These activities explore the initial sounds of words and encourage the children to notice the effect of the repetition of these sounds in poems.

Rats! (page 30) develops the children's ability to recognise the ways in which poets create particular effects by their choice of words. In this instance, several devices are combined, but the focus is on alliteration. Ask the children what sort of picture the poem creates in their minds. They could draw or paint the picture they imagine. Ask them what gives this impression; they might notice that many activities of the rats are described in just a few lines.

The scuttling and rushing of the rats are emphasised by the repetition throughout the verse of 's' sounds.

One weird week (page 31). The children should notice the repeated 's' sounds in the first line. Ask them which sound should be repeated in each of the other lines. This can be linked with word-level work on vocabulary and on phonemes and initial consonants.

Party poppers (page 32). The children could first make notes about parties: for example, games, foods, activities and things to wear, as well as descriptions of the atmosphere and what happens. They could take turns to add an alliterative noun to a descriptive word: for example, 'moaning Mum', 'grinning Grandad'.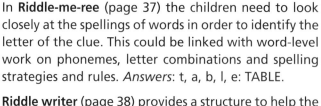

Humorous verse

Here the children are encouraged to enjoy nonsense poems as well as poems which explore words and ideas, and to play tricks with tongue-twisters and riddles.

Nonsense poems (page 33) presents a poem written purely for fun. The activity provides the children with a structure for a nonsense poem in the style of the example on the page. Draw attention to the details about real birds which are included (feathers and nest). Provide pictures of fish and discuss what they look like and what they do (and what they *don't* do), where they live (and where they don't live). With the children, compile a word-bank.

Freeze, froze, sneeze, snoze (page 34) could be linked with sentence-level work on the construction of past tenses. The children could look for patterns in the formation of past tenses and find any which do not fit the patterns: for example: grow/grew, know/knew, (but not glow/glew).

Ask a silly question (page 35) begins with an example from an anonymous poem. Read it to the children:

> The man in the wilderness
>   Asked of me
> How many strawberries
>   Grew in the sea.
>
> I answered him
>   As I thought good,
> As many as herrings
>   Grew in the wood.

Riddle match (page 36) develops the children's ability to look at things from different points of view. Some children might be able to think of riddles based on dual meanings of words: for example, tongue (of a person or a shoe) and eye (of a person or a needle). *Answers*: 1A, 2D, 3F, 4B, 5C, 6E. The answer to the riddle in the extension activity is: your reflection.

In **Riddle-me-ree** (page 37) the children need to look closely at the spellings of words in order to identify the letter of the clue. This could be linked with word-level work on phonemes, letter combinations and spelling strategies and rules. *Answers*: t, a, b, l, e: TABLE.

Riddle writer (page 38) provides a structure to help the children to write riddles.

Tongue-twister kit: 1 and 2 and **Twister writer** (pages 39–41) could be linked with work on alliterative patterns, but the essential difference between the two should be pointed out: poets use alliteration to create effects and feelings, whereas tongue-twisters are mainly for fun. Ask the children which tongue-twisters they find the most difficult to say quickly, and discuss which phonemes are difficult to say when they follow one another closely: for example, 'r' and 'w', 'ch' and 'sh', 's' and 'sh'.

Word-juggler jokes (page 42) presents the kinds of jokes which children tell one another. *Answers*: 1. Be quiet while I'm spooking. 2. Up his sleevies! 3. Tweethearts!; Mount Cleverest, The Ghost Office, Oinkment, Stable tennis.

Theme and meaning

This section focuses on poems for personal and class anthologies; it develops the children's skills in classifying poems by theme or subject and by poet, and in comparing poems on the same theme and by the same poet. It encourages the children to express their responses to poems.

Anthology: animal poems 1 (page 43). Ask the children if they can work out the meanings of the words crag and azure. Model how to find the words in a dictionary. The children could find examples of alliteration in the poem and describe the effect they create.

Anthology: animal poems 2 (page 44) presents another poem about an animal but with a completely different atmosphere from the one on page 43. This time the birds are not presented as powerful: they seem busy and cheerful. The children should notice the fast rhythm of the poem and the words used to create the impression of ducks splashing. Ask the children what effect the exclamation marks create.

Anthology: nature and **Anthology: the sea** (pages 45–46) provide formats on which the children can collect an anthology of evocative lines from poems.

I like this poem (page 47) can be used by the children to review any poems they like. (The page could be adapted for any poems they don't like.)

A poet (page 48) provides a structure to help the children to think about specific aspects of the work of a significant children's poet.

The horseman

- **Say the poem.**
- **Underline the rhyming words.**

 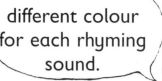
Use a different colour for each rhyming sound.

The Horseman

I heard a horseman
Ride over the hill;
The moon shone clear,
The night was still;
His helm was silver,
And pale was he,
And the horse he rode
Was of ivory.

Walter de la Mare

Now try this!

- **Learn the poem.**

Look and read   Cover   Say   Check

- **What helps you to remember the words?**
- **Write the poem on the back of this sheet.**
- **Have you remembered it correctly?** ✓
  Check

Teachers' note Read the poem with the children. Explain that 'helm' was a word used for 'helmet'. Re-read it and ask them to listen for anything which makes the poem easy to memorise. If necessary, emphasise the alliterative 'h' sounds in 'heard', 'horseman' and 'hill', and the end-of-line rhymes. The children could read the poem aloud in parts, each group reading two lines.

Developing Literacy
Poetry Year 2
© A & C Black 2001

The witches' spell 1

- **Say the witches' spell.**

This is from a play called *Macbeth* by William Shakespeare. There were three witches.

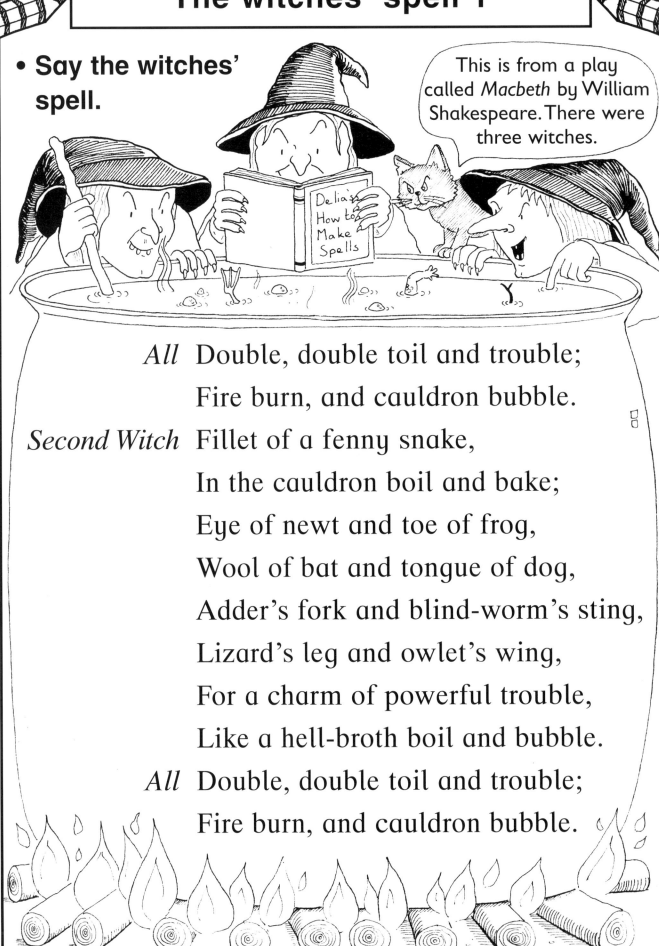

All Double, double toil and trouble;

Fire burn, and cauldron bubble.

Second Witch Fillet of a fenny snake,

In the cauldron boil and bake;

Eye of newt and toe of frog,

Wool of bat and tongue of dog,

Adder's fork and blind-worm's sting,

Lizard's leg and owlet's wing,

For a charm of powerful trouble,

Like a hell-broth boil and bubble.

All Double, double toil and trouble;

Fire burn, and cauldron bubble.

Teachers' note The poem could be read aloud two or three times, with groups taking turns to read the words of the Second Witch and the whole class reading the words spoken in chorus by all three witches.

**Developing Literacy
Poetry Year 2**
© A & C Black 2001

The witches' spell 2

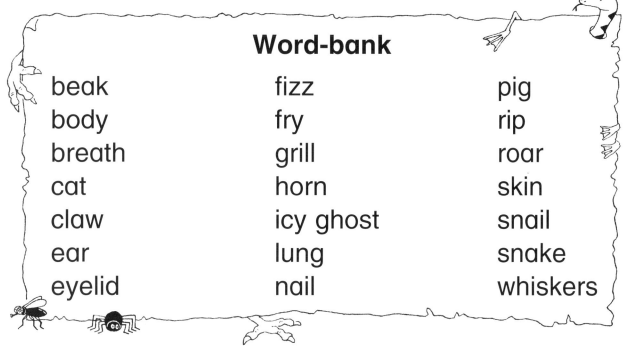

Word-bank

beak	fizz	pig
body	fry	rip
breath	grill	roar
cat	horn	skin
claw	icy ghost	snail
ear	lung	snake
eyelid	nail	whiskers

• **Write a spell for the First Witch. Fill in the gaps.**

First Witch   <u>Body</u> of a blue-black fly,

In the cauldron roast and _____;

Slime of _____ and _____ of goat,

Skin of _____ and _____ of stoat,

Vulture's _____ and weasel's _____,

Beetle's _____ and lion's _____,

For a charm of powerful trouble,

Like a hell-broth boil and bubble.

Now try this !

• **List some things for the Third Witch's spell. Use the word-bank to help you.**

Think of horrible things.

Teachers' note The children should first complete the activity on page 10. Encourage them to re-read *The Witches' Spell* from *Macbeth* while completing this page, to help them decide where the rhymes should be and to match their own 'spells' to the rhythm of the original. Their spells need not rhyme.

Developing Literacy
Poetry Year 2
© A & C Black 2001

Word-pictures 1

What pictures do you see when you read these words?

• **Write and draw.**

The words all come from real poems.

the forest's ferny floor	leaves a-shine with glistening drops of rain
A shady place in a forest, with ferns growing.	_____ _____ _____
a peacock with a fiery tail	(my sari) wraps round me like sunshine
_____ _____ _____	_____ _____ _____

Now try this!

• **Choose four** word-pictures **from poems you have read.**
• **Draw and label the pictures you see when you read them.**

Teachers' note Discuss evocative lines from poems the children have read (see **Introduction** page 6). Ask the children to describe the pictures that the lines conjure up. In the first example, ask them what the setting is, what they can 'see' there, what the atmosphere is like, the light, the colours and the sounds. Part of the description has been written; what can they add to it?

Developing Literacy Poetry Year 2
© A & C Black 2001

12

Word-pictures 2

- **Use this page to help you write a word-picture.**

What is your word-picture about?

Title

Notes

Use a thesaurus.

Use a dictionary.

Write your ideas and useful words.

Description

Write in sentences.

- **Underline the important words in your description.**

Word-picture

See how much you can say in a few words.

Teachers' note The children should first complete the activity on page 12. Provide a subject for them to write about: for example, a painting, a flower, or a picture of a waterfall, cliffs or standing stones. Discuss the impression it makes on them and help them to find words to write about it.

**Developing Literacy
Poetry Year 2
© A & C Black 2001**

Sad sounds, happy sounds

- **Read the words a few times.**
- **Do they sound sad or happy?**
- **Write** sad **or** happy **in the boxes.**

My heart aches, and a drowsy numbness pains
My sense…

Everyone suddenly burst out singing.

…her yellow
laughter spilling
over…

We are like birds
with a broken wing.

…all at once I saw a crowd,
A host, of golden daffodils:
Beside the lake, beneath the trees,
Fluttering and dancing in the breeze.

Now try this!

- **Read the words again.**
- **Underline the sad or happy words in each sentence.**

Teachers' note Invite children who can to read the words while the others listen. Discuss the first extract and ask the children if they think it sounds sad or happy. Can they explain why? Which words are the most important in creating this feeling?

**Developing Literacy
Poetry Year 2
© A & C Black 2001**

Sad words, happy words

- **Sort the words into sad or happy words. Write them on the notepads.**

You could add other words which you find in poems.

broken	frisks	skip
cheer	glad	smiling
cold	no birds sing	sorrow
dancing	no one dances	sparkling
fallen	on my own	tearful
forlorn	singing	weeps

Sad words

Happy words

- **Choose a happy and a sad poem for a class anthology .**
- **Copy the poems in your best writing.**

Teachers' note The children should first complete the activity on page 14. Point out that they should include pairs or groups of words as well as single words: for example, 'no birds sing' sounds sad, but 'singing' sounds happy.

**Developing Literacy
Poetry Year 2
© A & C Black 2001**

Poets' words

Sometimes poets make up words.
- Cut out the cards.
- Match each word to its meaning.

Poets' words

crash-flash	eye-stretcher	glubbery
gratty	moan-faced	neat meat
ping-string	puff-fluff	slithy
snappermouth	wig-wag	yackle

Meanings

beefburger	cotton wool	crocodile
elastic	miserable	scratchy
slippery and slimy	sticky and oozing	surprise
tail	talk too much	thunderstorm

Now try this!

- **What do you think these made-up words mean?**

scrabby	flump	raggled

Teachers' note Introduce the activity by discussing words which describe the things they name, such as flip-flops, stick insect and bluebell, and invite the children to name others (they could prepare this for homework). During the plenary session, they could share the meanings they thought of for the words in the extension activity.

**Developing Literacy
Poetry Year 2**
© A & C Black 2001

Your own words

Imagine you don't know the names for these things. You can make up your own words!

• Write names which describe these things.

pricklebody	slimer	

• **Make up words for these things you do.**

Now try this!

| hurry | sleep | drink | waste time |

Teachers' note Discuss the examples which have been completed and ask the children to explain them. Model the third example: encourage the children to think about what a hammer does, how it is used and the sound it makes. During the plenary session, they could share the words they have invented. The words could be illustrated and displayed.

Developing Literacy
Poetry Year 2
© A & C Black 2001

Green poem

• **Read the poem.**

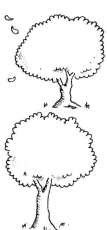

Green lettuce, green peas,

Green shade from green trees;

And grass as far as you can see,

Like green waves in a green sea.

Shirley Hughes

Here is another green poem.
It has the same pattern.

• **Fill in the gaps. Use the words from the box.**

floor	pond	lime	cabbage	carpet

Green _____, green _____,

Green _____ with green slime;

And moss across a rolling moor,

Like a green _____ on a green _____.

• **List six more green things.**
• **Re-write the first two lines of the poem. Use words from your list.**

Teachers' note Read the poem aloud and ask the children which words rhyme. Read it again, omitting the words 'trees' and 'sea'. Invite the children to supply them. Then read the second poem and the words in the box, and ask where each word could go. On an enlarged copy, record the children's ideas and invite them to read the completed verse aloud. Does it sound right? 'Green Lettuce, Green Peas' from *Colours* © 1986 Shirley Hughes.

Developing Literacy
Poetry Year 2
© A & C Black 2001

Red poem

- **List some red things.**

The pictures will help you to get started.

_____   _____

_____   _____

_____   _____

_____   _____

_____   _____

- **Write a red poem. Fill in the gaps with words from your list.**

Your poem need not rhyme.

Red _____, red _____,

Red _____ and red _____,

____ _____ and red _____,

____ _____ and red _____.

Now try this!

- **Say your poem.**
- **Underline any words that rhyme.**

Teachers' note The children should first complete the activity on page 18. This could be linked with work on colours: for example, by making a 'red corner' and collections of pictures of red things. Before the children do the activity, they could draw and write captions for red things. Ask them to say the names aloud. Provide a 'rhymes' word-bank from which they can choose words.

Developing Literacy
Poetry Year 2
© A & C Black 2001

Pattern poem

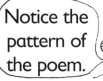

Notice the pattern of the poem.

- **Fill in the gaps in the poem.**
- **Draw a picture for the last verse.**

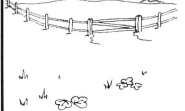

This is Farmer Fran's field.

This is the grass which grew in Farmer Fran's field.

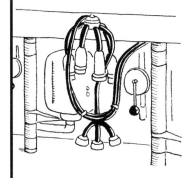

This is the cow which ate the grass which _____ _____ _____ _____ _____.

This is the machine which milked the cow which _____

_____

_____.

This is _____

_____

_____

_____

_____.

Now try this!

- **Write another** pattern poem **.**
  You can begin with any of these.

| This is Sean's shed | This is Clare's car | This is Tom's toy box |

Teachers' note The children could first read the nursery rhyme *The House that Jack Built* so that they can model their poems on it. They should notice that each verse begins by introducing something new and then linking it to the thing introduced in the previous verse. Some children might be able to continue the poem on another sheet of paper.

20

Developing Literacy
Poetry Year 2
© A & C Black 2001

Chat poem

- **Fill in the gaps. Write the name of an animal or a greeting. Follow the rhyming pattern.**

The pictures will give you clues.

Animal Chat

buffalo

polar bear

"See you later, alligator."

"In a while, <u>crocodile</u>."

"Hello, _____."

"_____, butterfly."

cow

"Take care, _____."

"_____, blue jay."

fly

kangaroo

"Bye for now, brown _____."

"How do you do, _____?"

"Hi, _____."

"Good luck, little _____."

crocodile

duck

Now try this!

- **Make up an animal chat poem using these.**

| Of course | That's nice | Cheerio |

Teachers' note Begin by reciting some of the words of the song *See You Later, Alligator* (see **Introduction** page 7). Ask the children to think of words and phrases that people often use in conversation: for example, 'Hello,' and 'Bye for now'. Can they think of animals' names which rhyme with them? The children can take turns to recite the completed lines to a partner.

**Developing Literacy
Poetry Year 2
© A & C Black 2001**

The way you say it 1

**Counting sheep can be boring!
Some shepherds have made up their
own numbers, for fun.**

- **Read this shepherds' boxed[counting poem] .**

Yan, tan, tether, mether, pimp.

Sether, hether, hother, dother, dick.

Yan dick, tan dick, tether dick,
    mether dick, bumfit.

Yan bumfit, tan bumfit, tether
    bumfit, mether bumfit, gigot.

Anonymous

• **Make up words to fill the gaps.**

Eeg, teeg, teeger, _____, _____.

Saggle, _____, _____, _____, tag.

Eeg tag, _____ tag, _____ tag, _____ _____,
    tackit.

Eeg tackit, _____ tackit, _____ _____,
    _____ _____, _____.

• **Write another counting poem using
numbers you have made up.**

Teachers' note Make an enlarged copy of the poem only. Invite children in turn to read it while
the others listen. Then ask them to read it as if the words were numbers. What difference do the
others notice? Read out lists of words, including series of numbers in other languages, using a
'counting' rhythm for some but not others. See if the children can say when you are 'counting'.

**Developing Literacy
Poetry Year 2**
© A & C Black 2001

The way you say it 2

Any words can sound like numbers if you say them as if you are counting.

- **Say these words.**

> Walk, talk, think, fall, find.
>
> Sing, settle, aim, nod, take.

Try to sound as if you are counting.

- **Fill in the gaps.**
- **Say the words as if you are counting.**

These are words for foods.

Jam, tea, _____, _____, _____.
_____, sausage, _____, _____, _____.

These are parts of the body.

Leg, toe, _____, _____, _____.
_____, ankle, _____, _____, _____.

These are colours.

Red, blue, _____, _____, _____.
_____, _____, _____, _____, _____.

Now try this!

How can you make higher numbers?

- **Write the next two lines for each person.**

You could add a word to each 'number'.

Teachers' note The children should first complete the activity on page 22. Read the counting poem again, asking them to notice how many 'numbers' there are in each line. The children should think about how many syllables there are in each 'number'. With a partner, they can read aloud the lines they have written. Does it sound as though they are counting?

Developing Literacy
Poetry Year 2
© A & C Black 2001

Aliens' alphabet

- **Make up names for the missing letters in the aliens' alphabet.**

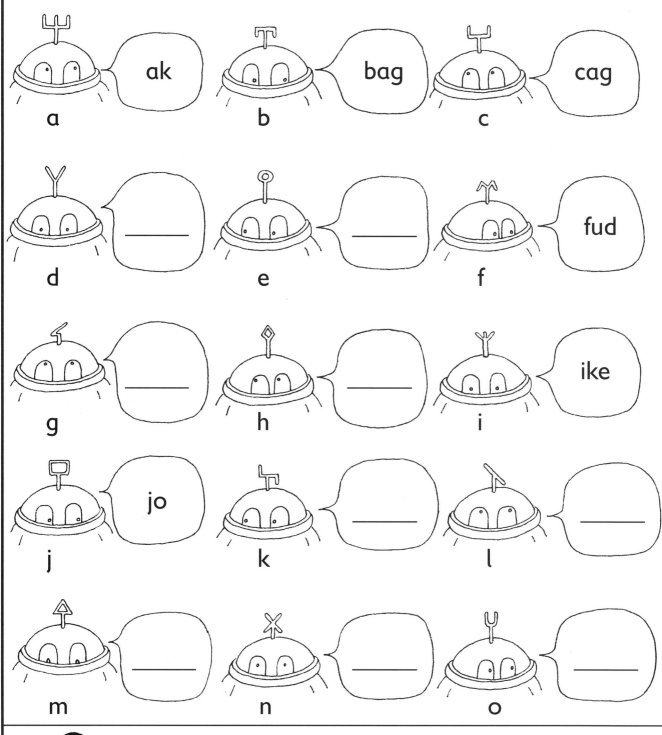

a — ak

b — bag

c — cag

d — ____

e — ____

f — fud

g — ____

h — ____

i — ike

j — jo

k — ____

l — ____

m — ____

n — ____

o — ____

Now try this!

- **Write the rest of the aliens' alphabet.**
- **Say it aloud.**

Teachers' note The children should make up letter names which have the same number of syllables ('beats') as the letters of the alphabet. Ask them which is the only letter with more than one syllable (w). Some children might be able to continue the aliens' alphabet so that the letters rhyme in the same sequence as the real alphabet.

Developing Literacy
Poetry Year 2
© A & C Black 2001

The drum

- **Say the poem.**
  Listen to the rhythm.
- **Draw a cross** ⊠ **above each** |beat| .

Some words might have two beats.

De Beat

X   X   X   X

De beat of de drum
    is a living heart

De skin of de drum
    is a living goat

De wood of de drum
    is a living tree

De belly of de drum
    is de call of de sea

De dum of de drum is me

Grace Nichols

Now try this!

- **Say the poem while your friend beats a drum.**
- **Check that the crosses are right.**

Take turns as readers and drummers.

Teachers' note Read the poem aloud, then re-read it with the children quietly beating drums, tapping tambourines or tapping their knees or the table-tops. Ask them how the words 'de drum' and 'de beat' help to create the rhythm of the poem. What difference would it make if they were changed to 'the beat' and 'the drum'?

**Developing Literacy
Poetry Year 2
© A & C Black 2001**

 Up and down,

up and down,

 Heel and toe,

heel and toe,

 Tap your knee,

tap your knee,

 Clap your hands,

clap your hands,

 Hoppety hop,

hoppety hop,

 Crissy cross,

crissy cross,

 Spin around,

spin around,

 Left and right,

left and right,

 Out and in,

out and in,

 Shake a leg,

shake a leg,

 Sing a song,

sing a song,

 Dance a jig,

dance a jig,

Teachers' note Introduce some of the rhyming pairs as a skipping rhyme: 'Up and down, up and down, / All the way to London town. Heel and toe, heel and toe, / All the way to Jericho'. Two children could turn a rope while another skips and does the actions (see **Introduction** page 7). Continued on page 27.

Developing Literacy
Poetry Year 2
© A & C Black 2001

Rhyme match 2

 All the way

to London Town.

 All the way

to Jericho.

 All the way

to the Red Sea.

 All the way

to Blundellsands.

 All the way

to the bus stop.

All the way

to Wester Ross.

 All the way

to Plymouth Sound.

 All the way

to the Isle of Wight.

All the way

to King's Lynn.

 All the way

to Winnipeg.

 All the way

to Hong Kong.

 All the way

to Castlerigg.

Teachers' note See also page 26. Copy the rhyme cards on this page and those on page 26 on to card of different colours. The children begin each pair of lines of the skipping rhyme with a card from page 26 and complete it with a card from this page. They could make up other cards to add to the rhyme.

Developing Literacy
Poetry Year 2
© A & C Black 2001

Hump, jump, wiggle, jiggle

- **Say the poem.**
- **Circle the rhyming words.**

Use a different colour for each sound.

Jump or Jiggle

Frogs jump

Caterpillars hump

Worms wiggle

Bugs jiggle

Rabbits hop

Horses clop

Snakes slide

Seagulls glide

Mice creep

Deer leap

Puppies bounce

Kittens pounce

Lions stalk –

But –

I walk!

Evelyn Beyer

How do other animals move?
- **Write an animal in each gap.**

_____ walk

_____ nod

_____ spring

_____ stalk

_____ plod

_____ swing

Teachers' note Read the poem aloud, emphasising the rhyming words. Repeat it with the children joining in. Cover the words for the animals' movements and ask the children to recite the poem, including the missing words. For the extension activity, point out that the animals do not need to rhyme with, or begin with the same letter as, their actions.

**Developing Literacy
Poetry Year 2
© A & C Black 2001**

Crash, dash, rumble, tumble

How do these animals move?

• **Choose words from the word-bank.**

Use a dictionary.

cows	_____	dragonflies	_____
deer	_____	hedgehogs	_____
goats	_____	tortoises	_____
rats	_____	greyhounds	_____
lambs	_____	hares	_____
ducks	_____	swallows	_____

Word-bank

amble	dip	scrabble
dabble	flash	start
dart	gambol	stroll
dash	roll	trip

• **Put the animals and movements in rhyming pairs.**

Now try this!

_____   _____

_____   _____

_____   _____

_____   _____

_____   _____

Teachers' note The children should first complete the activity on page 28. They should look up any new words. In the first activity, encourage them to choose the words that best describe the animals' movements, regardless of rhyme. In the extension activity, they need to consider rhyme.

**Developing Literacy
Poetry Year 2
© A & C Black 2001**

Rats!

- **Say the poem. Listen to the first sounds of the words.**
- **In each line, underline the words with the same starting sound.**

Rats!

They fought the dogs and killed the cats,

   And bit the babies in the cradles,

And ate the cheeses out of the vats,

   And licked the soup from the cooks' own ladles,

Split open the kegs of salted sprats,

Made nests inside men's Sunday hats,

And even spoiled the women's chats,

   By drowning their speaking

   With shrieking and squeaking

In fifty different sharps and flats.

From *The Pied Piper of Hamelin* by Robert Browning

Now try this!

- **Say the poem again. Listen to the** | consonant | **sounds.**
- **Which do you hear the most often?** ☐
- **Circle this sound in the poem.**

Work with a partner.

Developing Literacy
Poetry Year 2
© A & C Black 2001

Teachers' note Read the poem and ask the children what they notice about the sounds in some lines (repeat the first line, emphasising the 'k/c' sounds of 'killed' and 'cats'). Can the children find repeated sounds at the beginnings of words in any other lines? For the extension activity, the children should read the poem aloud while a partner listens, and vice versa.

One weird week

- **Fill in the gaps in the poem.**

Listen to the starting sounds.

One Sunny Sunday I saw a Snail;
One mad Monday I m_____ a m_____ ;
One t_____ Tuesday I t_____ a t_____ ;

made met model	wet watched walked
monster	whale wing went
teeming terrible toad	Wales to
tickled trout tried	thanked thief thistle
	threw thundery a

One w_____ Wednesday I w_____ _____;
One th_____ Thursday I _____ _____;

One _____ Friday I _____ _____;

One _____ _____ _____;

a fair to fairy found
funny fish foggy
to sad saw stormy
snowy Saturday
Spain sailed spider

- **Make up another weird week poem.**

Now try this!

Developing Literacy
Poetry Year 2
© A & C Black 2001

Party poppers

- **Finish the pairs of party words.**
  Their first sounds must be the same.

broken
biscuits

crackly
_____

_____
games

jiggly
_____

_____
sandwiches

_____
lollipops

_____
toys

burst
_____

_____
presents

_____
sweets

cheering
_____

giggling
_____

_____'s
birthday

- **Make up some word-pairs about food.**
  Example: | chewy chocolate |

Teachers' note Model the first four word-pairs (the first one has been completed), inviting the children to supply words which begin with the same sound: for example, broken biscuits, crackly crisps, great games, jiggly jelly.

Developing Literacy
Poetry Year 2
© A & C Black 2001

Nonsense poems

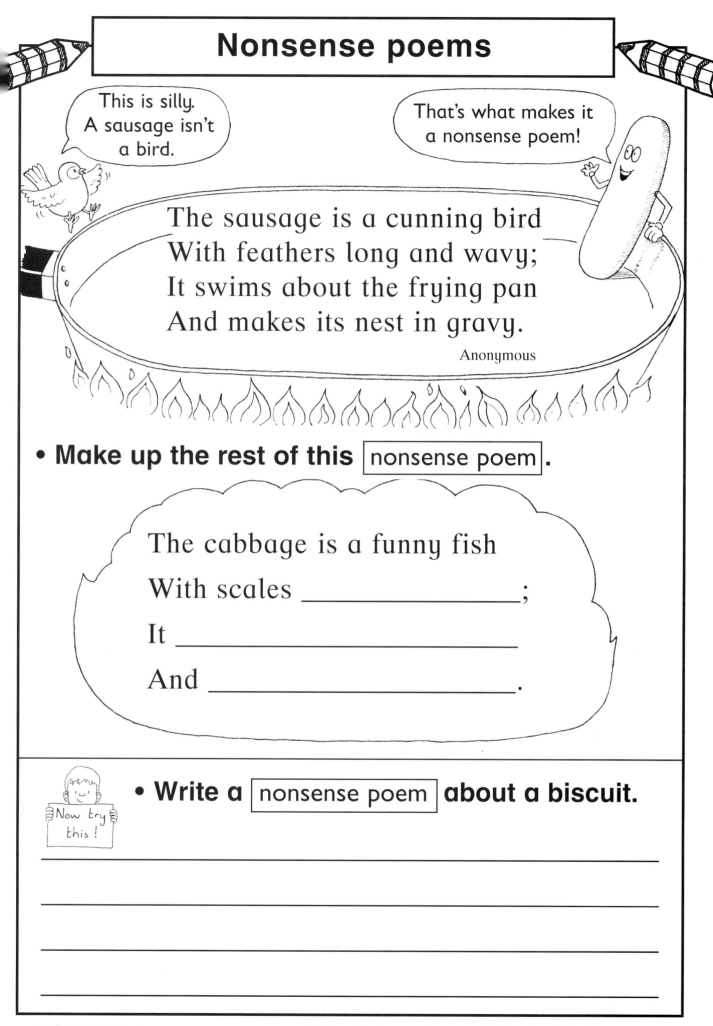

This is silly. A sausage isn't a bird.

That's what makes it a nonsense poem!

The sausage is a cunning bird
With feathers long and wavy;
It swims about the frying pan
And makes its nest in gravy.

Anonymous

• **Make up the rest of this** nonsense poem **.**

The cabbage is a funny fish

With scales _____;

It _____

And _____.

Now try this!

• **Write a** nonsense poem **about a biscuit.**

_____

_____

_____

_____

Teachers' note Introduce nonsense poems as poems which do not make sense ('non-sense'). Ask the children to point out any words which could be changed so that the poem *would* make sense (sausage, frying pan and gravy). In pairs, they could write a poem that does make sense, then change some of the words to turn it into a nonsense poem. The poems need not rhyme.

Developing Literacy
Poetry Year 2
© A & C Black 2001

Freeze, froze, sneeze, snooze

- **Read the poem. Circle the word that the poet made up.**

Ode to a Sneeze

I sneezed a sneeze into the air,

It fell to earth I know not where,

But hardened and froze the looks of those

In whose vicinity I snoze.

Anonymous

- **Make up some words of your own.**

freeze	froze	>	sneeze	snoze
speak	spoke	>	creak	
drink	drank	>	blink	
ride	rode	>	hide	
fly	flew	>	try	
shake	shook	>	make	
give	gave	>	live	

Now try this!

- **Make up four more words.**
- **Write a four-line poem which uses your words.**

Teachers' note Introduce the words 'ode' and 'vicinity' and let the children practise saying them. Discuss the ways in which verbs are changed to make the past tense: 'freeze'/'froze' (but not 'sneeze'/'snoze'); 'catch'/'caught' (but not 'match'/'maught') and so on.

Developing Literacy Poetry Year 2 © A & C Black 2001

Ask a silly question

- **Write nonsense answers to the nonsense questions.**

How many strawberries grow in the sea?

As many as herrings grow in the wood.

Where do daffodils wash their feet?

In the place where roses comb their _____.

When do worms buy new shoes?

On the day when caterpillars buy _____ _____.

How do sausages tell the time?

In the same way that _____ _____.

What do elephants wear to a party?

The same as _____ _____.

Now try this!

- **Write three nonsense questions for a partner to answer.**

Teachers' note As a whole-class activity, play a 'silly question and answer' game in which you (or a child) ask a silly question which invites a silly, but corresponding, answer: for example, 'How do fish brush their teeth?' / 'In the same way that snails comb their hair,' and so on.

Developing Literacy
Poetry Year 2
© A & C Black 2001

Riddle match

• **Match the** riddles **to the answers.**

Riddle	1	2	3	4	5	6
Answer	A					

1 What is black and white and read?

2 What is yours but is used mainly by other people?

3 What has a bed on which no one sleeps?

A a newspaper

B water

C a bar of soap

D your name
_____

E a bell

F the sea

4 What runs but has no legs?

5 What gets smaller as it gets older?

6 What has a ring but no finger?

• **Work out the answer to this riddle.**

Now try this!

I look the same as you;
You look the same as me.
When I see you, you see me.
I do whatever you do,
But my right is the left of you.

Anonymous

Teachers' note Read other examples of riddles to the children and help them to work out the answers. Encourage them to think of several possible answers for each riddle and then to choose the one that is the best match.

Developing Literacy
Poetry Year 2
© A & C Black 2001

Riddle-me-ree

Each line of the riddle tells you one letter of the answer.

- **Write the letters.**
- **Write the answer.**

The last line gives you a clue.

Riddle	Letter
Look once in roast and twice in toast,	t
Then in bacon and in taken,	
Then in baking but not in taking.	
My fourth is in lamb but not in ham;	
My fifth and last is in least but not last,	
And I'll come to your feast but not your fast.	

Answer _____

Now try this!

- **Write one-line riddles for these letters.**

Use pairs of words which go together, like sing and sang.

a _____

b _____

d _____

e _____

Teachers' note The children should first have experience of reading and working out riddles and should have completed the activity on page 36. Explain that this page is about riddles which spell a word. Point out that some lines offer more than one possible answer; the children should write down all the possibilities and wait until they have all the others before deciding which is correct.

Developing Literacy
Poetry Year 2
© A & C Black 2001

Riddle writer

- **Write a riddle to spell** drum .
- **Make up a clue for the last line.**

You could use some of these words.

Word-bank

any	dog	her	many	rung
black	down	him	meat	sing
blue	eat	hog	out	street
car	few	horse	rat	sung
cart	go	in	ring	up
come	goat	lane	road	van

My first is in dog, but not in _____

My second is _____

_____

My third is _____

_____

My fourth is _____

_____

Clue _____

Now try this !

- **Write a riddle for another word.**
- **Give it to a partner to solve.**

Teachers' note The children should first have experience of reading and working out riddles and should have completed the activities on pages 36 and 37. Encourage them to choose pairs of words for each line which go together in some way (such as 'horse' and 'cart').

**Developing Literacy
Poetry Year 2**
© A & C Black 2001

Tongue-twister kit 1

Rory licked a lolly;

A wicked worker walked to Wales;

A rabbit lived in a warren;

A green goblin gobbled gooseberries

Ten tired travellers talked

The bull bellowed at Brenda

Quickly count the questions

Winnie wore bright red wellies

Twelve treacle tarts

Nicola knitted with nine needles

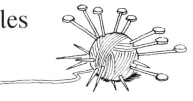

She sold sausages

Jack jiggled a jelly;

Teachers' note Cut out the cards (which could be copied on to card and laminated for re-use). The second part of each tongue-twister is on a card on page 40. The children match the halves and say the tongue-twisters. Continued on page 40.

**Developing Literacy
Poetry Year 2
© A & C Black 2001**

Tongue-twister kit 2

The lolly Rory licked was lime.

From Wick to Wrexham the worker walked.

A wild rabbit with waggling whiskers.

Growing on a green gooseberry bush.

As they trekked two by two on the track.
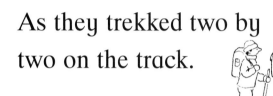

But brave Brenda bellowed back.

In the Queen's Christmas quiz.

For riding in wet weather.

Trickled treacle on the table.

But her knitting was knotty and never neat.
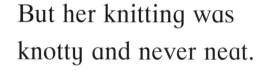

In the sausage shop.

Jack jogged to Japan.
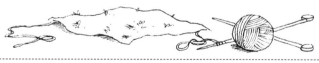

Teachers' note Continued from page 39. During the plenary session, ask the children which phoneme makes each tongue-twister difficult to say.

Developing Literacy
Poetry Year 2
© A & C Black 2001

- **Circle the tongue-twisting sounds.**
- **Complete each tongue-twister. Use the same sounds.**

Felicity Fettler, forty and fit
Feasted with fifty fortunate ferrets.

Deepak's dog dug deep

_____

Betty Buckle bought a bucket

_____

Seven spinning spiders

_____

Charlie chased chickens

_____

Bella bought broken bricks

_____

Shelley saw a shiny shoe

_____

I see icicles

_____

Now try this!

- **Choose one of the tongue-twisters.**
- **Write three more lines.**

Teachers' note The children should first complete the activities on pages 39 and 40. Model the first example with them and ask them which sounds they should repeat (the 'f' sound at the beginning of a word and the 't' sound at the end or in the middle).

Developing Literacy
Poetry Year 2
© A & C Black 2001

Word-juggler jokes

• Join the questions to the answers.

Answers

1. What did the mother ghost say to her son while she was talking on the telephone?

Tweethearts!

Be quiet while I'm spooking.

Up his sleevies!

2. Where did the general keep his armies?

3. What do you call two birds kissing?

• Change the words to make funny answers.

What is the world's brainiest mountain?

_____

Mount Everest

Where do spooks buy stamps?

_____

The Post Office

What do pigs put on cuts?

_____

Ointment

What is a horse's favourite game?

_____

Table tennis

Now try this !

• Write two more word-juggler jokes.
• Try them out on a partner.

Teachers' note Discuss the jokes with the children and ask them to point out the ways in which words have been changed: for example, sweethearts/tweethearts and speaking/spooking. In the second part of the activity, encourage the children to think of ways to alter the words.

**Developing Literacy
Poetry Year 2
© A & C Black 2001**

The Eagle

He clasps the crag with crooked hands;

Close to the sun in lonely lands,

Ringed with the azure world, he stands.

The wrinkled sea beneath him crawls;

He watches from his mountain walls,

And like a thunderbolt he falls.

Alfred, Lord Tennyson

- **Tick the correct answer.**
- **Write the words from the poem which tell you.**

1. The eagle is | gentle | | powerful | | mean |

_____

2. The eagle is | in a high place | | in a low place | | in a small place |

_____

3. The eagle is | with one other eagle | | in a group | | alone |

_____

4. The sea is | rough and stormy | | still | | rippling with small waves |

_____

- **Describe the eagle in your own words.**

Teachers' note Read the poem aloud while the children follow it on their own copies. Ask the children to describe the eagle, including what it does, and how. From where do they feel they are watching the scene? Do they notice the descriptions which make the reader feel as if he or she is sharing the eagle's view, looking down on to the sea below?

Developing Literacy
Poetry Year 2
© A & C Black 2001

- **Underline the words which make the ducks seem busy.**
- **Draw a box around the verse with a slower** `rhythm` **than the others.**
- **Do the words on the chart sound** `fast` **or** `slow` **? Write** `F` **or** `S`.

up tails all	
a-quiver	
busy	
undergrowth	
larder	
cool and full and dim	
heads down	
tails up	
whirl and call	
a-dabbling	

Ducks' Ditty

All along the backwater,
Through the rushes tall,
Ducks are a-dabbling,
Up tails all!

Ducks' tails, drakes' tails,
Yellow feet a-quiver,
Yellow bills out of sight
Busy in the river!

Slushy green undergrowth
Where the roach swim –
Here we keep our larder,
Cool and full and dim.

Every one for what he likes!
We like to be
Heads down, tails up,
Dabbling free!

High in the blue above
Swifts whirl and call –
We are down a-dabbling,
Up tails all!

Kenneth Grahame

- **Make a glossary of the new words you learned from this poem.**

Teachers' note With the children, compare this poem and *The Eagle* (page 43), noticing the different rhythms (the stillness of the first one until the eagle dives, and the busyness of this one). Point out contrasting words, such as clasps/dabbling. Ask the children which parts of this poem imitate the rhythm of ducks dipping their heads under water and bobbing back again.

Developing Literacy
Poetry Year 2
© A & C Black 2001

44

- **These lines are from poems about nature.**
- **Write some more on the leaves.**

Write the title of the poem and the poet's name.

The Bush

The bush is sitting under a tree and singing.

Ojibwa, Native American

The Song of Solomon

The flowers appear on the earth;
The time of the singing of birds is come.

The Bible

Teachers' note You could enlarge this page for the children, or for display. Remind the children of poems about nature that they have read. Then select evocative lines from some poems and invite the children to choose their favourite lines from others. Encourage them to use contents pages and indexes of titles and first lines to find poems about nature in poetry books.

**Developing Literacy
Poetry Year 2
© A & C Black 2001**

- **These lines are from poems about the sea.**
- **Write some more on the shells.**

Write the title of the poem and the poet's name.

Sea Timeless Song

Sea timeless

Sea timeless

Grace Nichols

The Rime of the Ancient Mariner

The fair breeze blew, the white foam flew,

Samuel Taylor Coleridge

Teachers' note You could enlarge this page for the children, or for display. Remind the children of poems about the sea that they have read. Then select evocative lines from some poems and invite the children to choose their favourite lines from others. Encourage them to use contents pages and indexes of titles and first lines to find poems about the sea in poetry books.

**Developing Literacy
Poetry Year 2
© A & C Black 2001**

I like this poem

Title	Poet
Number of verses	Number of lines in each verse

What the poem is about

> You could list the words which tell you what the poem is about.

My favourite line

> Read the poem aloud. Listen to each line.

Why I like it

My favourite words	Why I like them

Teachers' note Have available a selection of poetry books. Introduce the activity by inviting the children to name poems they like, and to say why. Ask them to recite any parts they can remember, even one or two words. Re-read any poems they choose and ask them the name of the poet, the number of verses and so on.

Developing Literacy
Poetry Year 2
© A & C Black 2001

A poet

Poet's name _____

About the poet

Where was the poet born? Where does he or she live?

Poems I have read by this poet

My favourite

Topics which interest the poet

What does the poet often write about?

Anything special

Think about rhymes, other sounds, words.

Teachers' note Discuss a poet whose work the children have read at school. Help them to find information about the poet. Can they name any poems by him or her? What kind of things does the poet like to write about? Point out any special devices, such as alliteration, special use of punctuation, rhyme or invented words.

Developing Literacy
Poetry Year 2
© A & C Black 2001